on the cover:
portrait of Frederic Chopin
by Delacroix

on this page:
monument to Frederic Chopin
in Warsaw

Text by Adelaide Murgia

Translated from the Italian by C. J. Richards

Copyright © 1966 Arnoldo Mondadori Editore, S.p.A., Milan
English translation copyright © 1967 Arnoldo Mondadori
Editore, S.p.A., Milan

First published in Italian under the title I GRANDI DI TUTTI I TEMPI:
Chopin by Arnoldo Mondadori Editore S.p.A., Milan

This edition published by
Elite Publishing Corporation
11-03 46th Avenue
Long Island City, New York 11101

Originally published by
the Curtis Publishing Company

Library of Congress Catalog Card Number: 84-21131
ISBN: 0-918367-03-4

Printed and bound in Italy by Officine Grafiche
Arnoldo Mondadori Editore, Verona, Italy, October 1984.

CHOPIN

ELITE PUBLISHING CORPORATION

A LIFELONG NOSTALGIA FOR POLAND

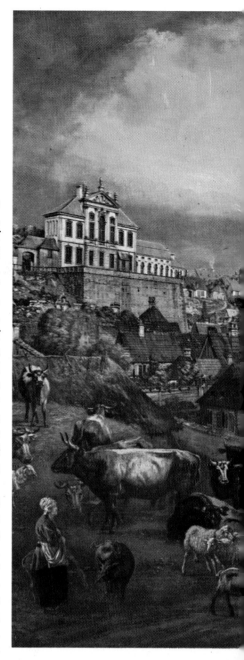

The first piece of music Chopin composed, when he was eight years old, was a polonaise; the last piece, a mazurka. These two compositions are indicative of the love for his homeland that was so often expressed in his music, although he chose to live as an exile. He left home one day at dusk, the hour of "zal" (Polish for homesickness). And, although he was to die of it in Paris, this homesickness was the very mainspring of his inspiration. Without this, a handful of his native soil, and the cherished portraits of those he left behind, he could not have carried on. Nor would he have gone on composing. Remoteness was the essence of his inspiration. Chopin found that in order to sustain life, he needed to look upon life as a mosaic from which certain pieces were missing, irretrievably lost in time. (Nietzsche's words could well be applied to him: "The magic of music is identified with the language of our past.")

The voluntary exile was a deeply patriotic Pole whose roots remained in his native province. When Chopin left Poland he took with him some of the anguish of a land constantly being overrun by armies. Throughout the centuries Poland had been the prey of its neighbours. It is to his credit that he never capitalized on his position as an exile, on his love for his homeland; he never played the part of national prophet, although he was urged on all sides to do so. In this respect he was unlike many of his contemporaries. No role could have been more alien to his nature. The great musician, who was destined to give such eloquent expression to homesickness in the musical patterns native to his country—polonaises and mazurkas—never attempted to do more than express his own feelings, his need to remember, his reasons for having left home. He recaptured the flavour of ancient Slavic legends in his ballades and in his last polonaises, Opus 44 (1841) and Opus 53 (1843). These are songs of love for his country in mourning, songs that have never been surpassed in their poignancy; but they were composed primarily for himself, not for others. The concept of national art—the vehicle for the feelings of a nation—does not allow for the solitary voice of the artist.

Portrait of Frédéric Chopin (*left*)
by Miroszewski. The son of a Polish
lady and of a French emigrant, Chopin
was born in Poland in 1810. He left
his home when he was about 20, never
to return. He settled in Paris, where
he lived for most of the rest of his
life. Keenly aware of his dual heritage
and of his uprooting, he suffered
perpetual pangs of homesickness.
His nostalgia for his birthplace lives
on in his music. Above: The Palace of
the Majority in Warsaw in a painting
by Bellotto (*at the National Museum*).

Opposite page: Catherine II of
Russia. The Empress, in collusion
with Prussia and Austria,
promoted the dismemberment of
Polish territory in successive
stages. These have come down
in history as the three partitions
of Poland (1772, 1793, 1795).
Thaddeus Kosciuszko (*bottom of
page*) was the leader of the
heroic and ill-fated Polish
revolution of 1794, which
was fought "not for the
nobility but for the freedom

of the whole nation." At
Raclavitz, with his regulars, he
held at bay the army of the
Empress. A perennial fugitive
and exile, he was always
on the side of the oppressed.
He gave the lands he had
been given as a present in
America to the Negroes. He
died in Switzerland in 1817 when
Chopin was seven years old.
Opposite page: Two old prints
of Wroclaw and Poznan,
the latter typically Polish.

Nicolas Chopin (below, left), father of Frédéric Chopin, was born in a village in Lorraine which, during the reign of Louis XV of France, was governed by the King's father-in-law, the Polish King Stanislas Leszczynski (Good King Stanislas). Nicholas left home in 1788 to seek his fortune in Poland. A self-taught, self-made man, a good violinist, he first became tutor to, among others, the future Maria Walewska, then professor of French at the Lyceum of Warsaw. Next to him: Justine Krzyzanowska, jokingly referred to as the lady majordomo, a poor relation in the house of Countess Skarbek at Zelazowa Wola where Nicholas and Justine met and were married in 1806, and where Frédéric Chopin was born. Right: Frédéric Skarbek, whose tutor Nicholas Chopin was from 1802-10; he was a noted economist as well as Frédéric Chopin's godfather. Opposite and below: the grounds and interior of the Skarbek villa. Today, enlarged and turned into a museum, it is used for concerts of Chopin's music.

REJOICING IN WARSAW

Nineteen years after the first partition of Poland—the dismemberment of her territory by Russia, Prussia and Austria—Easter of the year 1791 brought to the Polish people something more precious than this spring festival: a constitution. The nobles and the clergy had buried their differences and had come to an agreement vainly sought in the past. The sessions of the Diet in Warsaw had lasted for years. On this night the King, after having sworn to uphold the constitution, went forth in a great cortège to the cathedral to offer up a Te Deum of thanksgiving. The procession passed between the palaces that lined the Miodowa and the Krakowskie Przedmiescie, while torches threw their flickering light on the representatives of the arts and the nobles, all dressed in traditional costumes. Commoners and lords marched side by side, and the swords of Prince Joseph's hussars formed an arch of honour for Stanislas Augustus, "the King with the people, the people with the King." A crowd of more than 30,000 gathered in the square; its shouts echoed from street to street.

King Stanislas was noted for his ineptitude as a ruler. However, he made up for this, at least in part, by being a generous patron of the arts. True, he shirked governmental responsibility, but he redressed the balance by recruiting painters from far-flung capitals to immortalize the palaces, churches and wooden hovels that made up Warsaw. Even he was pleased by the agreement just reached, which seemed to bring back the Poland of a period when unity and just laws had made of it a state worthy of respect.

Among the cheering crowd there was a certain Nicolas Chopin, a French citizen. When he was 17 years old, impelled possibly by signs of revolution in France, he had left his native Vosges and his family of agricultural workers and carters, and had gone north. Nicolas, who had been living in Poland for several years, felt the joy of the Polish people as though it had been his own. No one, on this memorable night in Warsaw, could guess that the constitution through which Poland seemed at last to have found a united voice was, instead, to mark the beginning of years of bitterness and mourning.

A TUTOR SEEKS HIS FORTUNE

The Russian Empress was not pleased with the Polish constitution. She took a dark view of these impetuous Warsaw Jacobins, and of this Stanislas Augustus who encouraged them—a king, a former lover, and a perennial debtor to boot! The year 1795 was to mark the third and last partition of Poland. After this, the country ceased to exist as an entity, and Warsaw was swallowed up by Russia. Nicolas Chopin took part in the last revolutionary uprising of 1794 when Kosciuszko and his peasants, armed only with scythes, successfully withstood Catherine of Russia's cannon. He decided to settle permanently in Poland, despite the Russian occupation; he was never to see France again. He was an army officer for a time, then decided to become a tutor to earn his living: teachers of French were in great demand among good Poles, who expressed their resistance to Russian domination by cultivating the language of Western civilization.

In 1802 Nicolas was in Zelazowa Wola, a village six leagues from Warsaw, where he was a tutor to the Skarbek boys. Count Skarbek, a wastrel and *débauché,* lived abroad. A distant cousin, Justine Krzyzanowska, helped the Countess to run her estate. Years passed, and the French tutor became practically a member of the family. A talented and enthusiastic musical amateur, he played selections with Mademoiselle Justine during the long winter evenings when the neighbouring gentry gathered to gossip by the countess's fireside. Meanwhile, King Stanislas Augustus had died in Russia, unable to withstand for long the charity scornfully doled out by Catherine II. But a seed had taken root. The Polish soldiers who had enlisted in Italy under Napoleon had as a motto: "All free men are brothers." The Napoleonic storm gathered speed; unfortunately it went by without doing much good to Poland. Napoleon's last 5,000 Polish soldiers ended up in Santo Domingo, decimated by skirmishes with the natives and by malaria.

On June 2, 1806, Justine Krzyzanowska and Nicolas Chopin were married, and settled down in an annex of the Skarbek house. Their son, Frédéric, was born in Zelazowa Wola on February 22, 1810. A few months later, the family moved to Warsaw.

Left: The election of King
Stanislas Augustus of Poland,
detail of a painting by Bellotto
(in the Warsaw National Museum).
Elected in 1764, with the backing
of Russia, Stanislas Poniatowski
at first allowed the free practice
of all faiths, for Poland had been
torn by religious troubles and
dissent. But his liberalism only
served to stir the wrath of the Catholic
nobles, who set off a disastrous
civil war. The King was further
hampered by his inability to resist
the territorial claims of Russia,
Prussia and Austria. Despite
Kosciuszko's heroic defence, the
Russian Empress finally obliged
Stanislas to join the Confederation
of Targovica and to accept the
successive partitions of Poland
by the three powers. The weak
monarch died at St. Petersburg in
1798, a guest or prisoner of the
Czars. He was a great patron of
painters. Above: Church of the
Sisters of St. Bridget and the
Arsenal, where, in the school of
engineers, Nicolas Chopin, father
of Frédéric, taught French.
Opposite page, bottom: Two
caricatures of Polish plebeian
types done by Frédéric Chopin
when he was still a schoolboy.
Chopin never lost the taste for
caricature and for pantomime
which was shared by the
intellectuals of his era.
Opposite page, above: Greetings
dated December 6, 1816,
written on St. Nicolas' Day
for his father.

Felix Mendelssohn's sister Fanny played such an important part in his life that her name cannot be omitted from any biography of the musician from Hamburg. In the same way, Louise, Emily and Isabelle Chopin were an integral part of the life of their famous brother, who was deeply attached to them. Louise, the eldest (opposite page, above, left), born in 1807, taught him the first rudiments of French and of music. He opened his heart to her in his frequent letters. She also published, in collaboration with Isabelle (opposite page, above, right), a few "novels for the young". Emily (centre) was a talented girl who died of tuberculosis during her adolescence. The young Frédéric founded with her a "Society for Literary Diversion" (family reading and dramatics). Opposite below: The Lazienski Palace. Immediate right: Joseph Elsner, composer of operas, symphonies, and chamber music. He was also the founder of the Warsaw Conservatory, where Chopin took courses in musical composition. Next to him: Wojciech Zywny, a Czech, Chopin's only piano teacher. Although not himself at the top of his profession, Zywny must be credited for teaching Chopin to follow unwaveringly his own bent. Far right: Dominik Magnuszewski, romantic novelist and playwright. Above: Painting by Bellotto, the Krakowskie Przedmiescie and the Warsaw Conservatory, with a carriage leaving the Miodowa, or Honey Street.

10

A HAPPY HOME
FOR THE PRODIGY

The house of Nicolas Chopin, former accountant, former army officer and, from 1810 on, professor of French at the Warsaw Lyceum and at the Military School, was known throughout the city. Sometimes a small open carriage would stop in front of the house. The Russian General Kuruta would explain courteously each time that he had come by order of the Grand Duke to escort to the Bruhl Palace the young piano prodigy, Frédéric Chopin. Only this small boy's music had the power to dispel the fits of depression that seized the gloomy Constantine, brother of the Czar and commander-in-chief of the new Polish army. The "little Polish Mozart" was the talk of Warsaw. He was proudly shown off before dignitaries visiting the capital, from the Russian Czarina, Maria Teodorovna, to the Polish composer and friend of Goethe's, Maria Szymanowska, another bright star in the Polish firmament. The *Literary Journal* of February 1818 wrote about a polonaise by Frédéric Chopin, aged eight: "Geniuses are born in our country also, but the lack of publicity hides them from the public."

Chopin in his early youth showed a talent for caricature as well as for musical composition. He also had a taste for comedy, and staged several plays with his sister Emily as co-author and co-director. It was a happy childhood never to be forgotten: summers in Szafarnia, Christmas with "oplatki" (wafers traditionally served at this time) and honey: "May God grant that in a year we can again share the breaking of these wafers . . ." The Chopin house was always filled with people and music. On Mme Chopin's Thursdays, the young people danced while she played the piano. And in the drawing room, the regulars gathered: They played whist, and talked: about the Atheneum recently inaugurated in Warsaw; about the new Grand Duchy of Poland, whose titular head was the irascible Czar Alexander of Russia, against whom even Napoleon's Guard had broken. Then, in April 1821, Frédéric dedicated a farewell polonaise to his teacher Zywny, who said he had nothing more to teach him. They remained great friends. From 1823 to 1826, Chopin studied at the Warsaw Lyceum. This was another happy period of his life.

Princess Louise and Prince Anton Radziwill, in a print by Sintzenich. Chopin spent many pleasant summers in their castle, Antonin, where he played the piano with the feudal Prince, a great music lover (to whom he later dedicated a trio), and with his two daughters, Wanda and Elise. The latter did the profile, below, of Chopin at the piano.

A NEW STAR ON THE MUSICAL HORIZON

Heading the list of his youthful muses were Elise and Wanda Radziwill. He wrote about Wanda: "What a pleasure to place her little fingers on the keyboard!" But Costantia Gladkowska (right), an opera singer, was his first love. After Chopin had left the country in 1831, Costantia married the wealthy Joseph Grabowski. She soon became blind and ended her days in bitterness. She survived Chopin by 40 years.

Having finished his studies at the Lyceum in 1826, Chopin went on to the Warsaw Conservatory to complete his musical education. He worked hard at musical composition and at the same time started his sentimental education. In 1829 he went to Vienna; for some time Nicolas Chopin had been saving up for this trip which was to mark his son's real debut in the world of music. Vienna was then the official centre of artists and critics who wanted to make their mark in the world. The publisher Hans Haslinger had already set up in St. Stephen Square a large poster of the Polish pianist proclaiming "the new star of the north". Chopin didn't let this reception go to his head. He wrote home: "What reassures them is that I am not after their money and that I shall not request an honorarium." He had a tremendous success on August 11 at the Kaerntnerthor Theatre. Only one lady, in the first row, gave voice to her disappointment at the pianist's look of frailty; she plainly did not know that pallor was fashionable in romantic circles. A second concert was requested. This time the orchestra did not refuse to decipher his Variations, Op. 2 and the Krakowiak Rondo, Op. 14. It was a triumph. Lichnowsky, Beethoven's great friend, led the applause.

"An artist, unheralded, has appeared on the musical horizon much like a brilliant meteor," wrote the authoritative *Allgemeine Musikalische Zeitung*. Only one critic objected to those aspects of his technique which were to remain the hallmark of Chopin's piano playing: the delicacy of his touch, the softness of his tone, the lack of dash and brilliance much favoured by the public, and his indifference to the preferences of the audience. "Here they are accustomed to the loud blare of virtuosi, but this is my way of playing, and I know that artists and women like it," Chopin wrote.

The two concerts that Chopin gave in Warsaw the following year established him as Poland's most representative musician. This time he played the Concerto in F minor, Costantia's concerto; and Costantia Gladkowska, his first schoolboy love, blue-eyed and blonde, smiled at him from a box at the National Theatre. For once the opera singer was not surrounded by admiring junior Russian officers.

It was greatly to the credit of Stanislas Poniatowski that he had summoned to Warsaw Bernardo Bellotto, born in Venice in 1720, nephew and student of Antonio Canal, and known, like him, as Canaletto. Bellotto painted many views of Warsaw (above, a street scene), which are now in the National Museum of the Polish capital. He died in Warsaw in 1780. Left: The leaning tower and the house where Copernicus was born in Thorn; young Chopin visited them.

COSTANTIA AND TITUS

Ignatius
Dobrzynski

Angelica
Catalani

Casimir
Brodzinski

For Frédéric Chopin, aged 18, Costantia Gladkowska and Titus Woyciechowski were the two faces of one love. Love was the great preoccupation of the romantics. If it caused anguish—if it was attended by the pain of separation and renunciation—that only added to the flavour of the game. They all played at it: Musset, Foscolo, Heine, Witwicki, Byron. If one could not acquire the touching pallor of consumption, a proper combination of love and separation supplied the anguish necessary for artistic creativity. And, indeed, Chopin wrote a great deal of new music in this period: Variations Op. 2, number 3, Fantaisie Op. 13, the second Concerto. Suffering is a plant that must be cultivated if it is to flower. Costantia, his first love; Titus, the young athlete whom he had singled out at the Lyceum ("you, the most delightful", "you, the one I love best of all . . ."); the arranged meetings; the afterthoughts and the swoonings; all these were part of a comedy that had to be played out.

In 1830 Chopin decided to leave his homeland. He approached this step with mixed feelings. "Oh, Titus, how sad it must be not to die where one has lived!" he wrote. But on the other hand: "You are mistaken if you think that somewhere in some recess of my heart I want to remain here; you must know that I shall trample over everything that does not involve me." When the time came, he realized that he had to act quickly if he was not to let himself be persuaded to remain. On October 11, 1830, at the National Theatre in Warsaw, Chopin performed his Concerto in E Minor. During the second part of the concert Costantia sang, "Oh how many tears I have shed for thee!" an aria of Rossini's that might have been the theme song of their love. Chopin escorted her from the stage—already echoes from the past and visions of the future were merging. Then came wild, delirious applause. "This time," Chopin was to say, "the orchestra, the audience, I myself, everyone understood." After that there remained only one thing to do: leave. On November 2, 1830, a carriage stopped briefly for a farewell to Zelazowa Wola; his friends gave him as a present a fistful of Polish soil. Then the carriage sped on to Vienna via Kalisz and Dresden.

Top of the page: Ignatius Dobrzynski was a contemporary of Chopin, the greatest Polish symphony composer of the time. Angelica Catalani, a famous Italian singer, was on a tour in Poland when she heard the child prodigy, Chopin, play in a concert. She gave him a gold watch. Later, in Paris, she went to see him on his deathbed. Casimir Brodzinski was a leader of Polish romanticism, a poet and a critic. Antonia Bianchi, *who lived with Paganini from 1824 to 1828 and bore him a son, Achille. She appeared with Chopin in a concert in Warsaw. Samuel Linde was rector of the Warsaw Lyceum and author of a monumental dictionary of the Polish language. He helped the tutor Nicholas Chopin to become a professor of French. He also taught Frédéric Chopin. He caught him in class once doing a caricature of him, but all he did was to write in the margin: "Well drawn."*

Antonia
Bianchi

Samuel
Linde

Sofia
Zamoyska

Wojciech
Boguslawski

*Countess Sofia Zamoyska was
founder of the Warsaw Welfare
Society, and arranged Chopin's first
concert (when he was eight). The
poet Niemcewicz wrote a satire on it
in which the philanthropic ladies, in
order to attract attention to the
young prodigy, subtract so many
years from his age that in the end he is
carried on the stage by his wet nurse.*

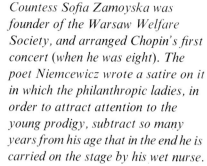

*The last of the portraits
shows Wojciech Boguslawski,
a former officer, who gave
Poland her national theatre.
He was extremely popular as
patriot, playwright and actor.
Opposite page: The Belvedere
and the Arsenal in Warsaw.
On this page, left: Painting
by Bellotto showing a
country house in Wilanow.
Above: A couple of citizens
of Poznan, a city familiar
to Chopin; and a barge in
the port of Danzig.*

Above: The castle of Ojcow, to which the young Chopin once tried to make an excursion, but lost his way in the night. Below: Pieskowa Skola, another somewhat romantic Polish scene, in a water colour by Vogel. Opposite page, top: Prague, the old city, a copper engraving by Axmann. In this "city of music lovers who are prepared to criticize even a Paganini," Chopin stayed briefly in 1829 on his way back from his triumphal debut in Vienna. He gave no concerts there. August Klengel, a successor to Bach in the art of the fugue, played for him at length. "He plays well, but I should have liked him to play better," commented Chopin, never lavish with praise for his colleagues.

THE VOICE OF A DEFIANT HOMELAND

Once he had crossed the border, Chopin's tension diminished and he calmly enjoyed the great separation. He was in top form when he improvised for the Court in Dresden. Titus caught up with him in Kalisz. The two friends reached Vienna on November 23, 1830. They rented an apartment in the Kohlmarkt. On the 29th unexpected news came from Poland: there had been an uprising of the people of Warsaw, and Grand Duke Constantine with his Cossacks had abandoned the city. The people of Poland were once more in arms, and were playing a card that again seemed to be their last. Titus Woyciechowski left Vienna to enlist. Chopin tried to follow him, but lost track of him on the outskirts of the city. He never saw him again.

Then a letter came from home: his father, guessing his uncertainties, begged him to do nothing rash, but to think only of his career. Witwicki, a few months later, was to point out to him: "You left in order to acquire glory for your country." Chopin suddenly found Metternich's Vienna suffocating. Strauss's cheerful waltzes drowned out Chopin's, which were filled with nostalgia and bitterness. Haslinger refused to buy his music. "Pay, you dog, I have no intention of letting you have it because of your charms," Chopin muttered. Despite his dissatisfaction, Chopin passed almost eight months in Vienna. He worked on Scherzo No. 20, skated, had his portrait done by young Hummel. He moved about in society, becoming friendly with Malfatti, the brilliant court doctor. He reviewed his past ("Did Costantia really love me or was she playing a part?"). Finally he left, his passport stamped with a visa for London. He went at a leisurely pace through Salzburg and Munich. In Stuttgart, on September 8, 1831, he heard that Warsaw was in Russian hands. The news inspired his Etudes Op. 10. The last Etude (No. 12), known as the *Revolutionary,* was written at one sitting. It was a masterpiece. The spirit of the Polish nation in chains was felt throughout the Western world. Chopin did not grab a gun and run to the last barricade, but he was for his compatriots the voice of a nation whose spirit was never conquered by the oppressor.

"She seems to exude from the stage a scent of fresh flowers which caresses her voluptuously. Her diminishing notes could not be more exquisite, her rising chromatic scales are superb," wrote Chopin about Henrietta Sontag (above) to his friend Titus Woyciechowski. And he added: "She has infinitely more grace off stage than on, although her conversation remains impersonal." The lively soprano, who gave a concert in Warsaw in 1830 for the visit of Nicholas I of Russia, was then barely 24 and at the peak of her glory. She had made her debut at six and had been a favourite of Beethoven and of von Weber before becoming the toast of Europe.

Above: St. Michael's Square and the National Theatre in Vienna. Paganini (far right, by Elise Radziwill) made his debut there on March 24, 1828. The tickets were expensive (10 florins), but the house was sold out and ecstatic at his playing. Even Schubert for once had a few gulden in his pocket and was able to buy a ticket. Urging his friend Bauernefeld to attend the next concert, he said, "I tell you, there will never again be such a man here!" And they went back together to hear the "divine, infernal Genoese". Right: The Cathedral of St. Stephen in Vienna.

Above: The Church of St. Peter and (below) the Karlsplatz, in Vienna. Chopin made his debut in that city on August 11, 1829. Beethoven had died in Vienna barely two years before; Haydn had sung in the choir of St. Stephen's; Mozart and Gluck had made Vienna their home and had composed many of their works there. After his success, Chopin was warmly welcomed by the Lichnowsky family, whose house was a meeting place for the intellectual elite. Prince Lichnowsky even offered Chopin, for his second concert, a piano on which Beethoven himself had played.

Below: Painting by Boilly, in the Louvre. It was from such a coach that Chopin alighted in Paris in September, 1831. "I shall certainly stay here longer than I had planned," he wrote. He soon became a frequent guest at Prince Adam Czartoryski's Mondays and at Count Plater's Thursdays (see below); Countess Plater said that

"had she been young and beautiful she would have chosen the pianist Hiller as friend, Liszt as lover and 'dear little Chopin' as husband." Below: Kalkbrenner, the German virtuoso whose reign in Paris seemed destined to last forever; and Count Kniaziewicz, a friend of Chopin's. Opposite: Charles X being crowned king of France (1824).

IN PARIS, "LIFE IS INTOXICATING"

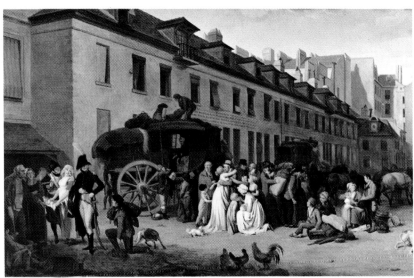

Adam Czartoryski

Friedrich W. Kalkbrenner

Louis Plater

Karol Kniaziewicz

Chopin's first lodgings in the capital of Louis Philippe was at 27 Boulevard Poissonnière, on the fifth floor. From here he had a splendid view of the Paris of 1831. It enchanted him. Here George Sand, the eccentric lady novelist, noted, "What a joy to be alive! In spite of troubles, husband, boredom, debts, family, petty gossip, life is intoxicating." Paris was cosmopolitan, the political refugee club of half of Europe. Here Poles could live in a congenial atmosphere. The Franconi troupe at the Olympia Club had a tremendous success with their elaborate review about Polish events. Paris was "a city," Chopin wrote to Titus, "where you can laugh, cry, have a good time, be bored, do what you want, no one looks at you, thousands of people do the same thing and each in his own way . . . a city where the Opera and musicians are the best in the world. . . ." The golden-voiced Rubini and La Malibran electrified audiences at the Opera. Rossini was the director of the Italian Theatre in Paris, Cherubini of the Conservatory; Liszt, Hiller, Herz were superlative pianists. And there was Kalkbrenner, the master of traditional piano-playing. This good German invited Chopin to put himself under his tutelage; in three years, he assured him, he would make of him something exceptional. "Chopin," he said, "plays very well if inspired, mediocrely if uninspired." Chopin retorted, "He never happens to be inspired: I don't want to become a copy of him . . . and many people think that it is conceit that makes him thrust his lessons on me so that later he can proclaim me his pupil. . . ." Elsner, in Warsaw, agreed—and so did his new friends: Liszt, the cellist Franchomme, young Mendelssohn. The Chopin-Kalkbrenner skirmish ended in a diplomatic draw. Chopin dedicated his Concerto in E minor to the German virtuoso, who returned the compliment, dedicating to the rising star a set of Variations (Op. 20) on a Mazurka of Chopin. In February, 1832, Chopin was one of the performers of Kalkbrenner's Grand Polonaise for six pianos, along with Hiller, Sowinski, Osborne, Stamaty and Kalkbrenner: a signal honour. "It is a crazy notion," Chopin wrote of the Polonaise. The Revue Musicale, however, accorded it an admiring reception.

POPULARITY AND
A TASTE FOR
ELEGANCE

A torrid summer, aggravated by an outbreak of cholera, darkened Chopin's bright prospects in Paris. High society was deserting the city, leaving its artists forlorn. The musician had taken to signing himself "Frédéric Chopin, poor devil", and thought of seeking his fortune in America. But the gods were watching over him. Walking along one of the boulevards one day, Chopin ran into an old friend, Valentin Radziwill, an uncle of Wanda and Elise, the muses of his adolescence. That very evening the drawing-room doors of James Rothschild's elegant town house were thrown open to the young Pole. Chopin improvised. It took only a few minutes to make Paris society realize that it could not get along without Frédéric Chopin. The first to ask him for piano lessons was his hostess. Four lessons a day paid well enough to free him from the slavery of concert tours, which not only distracted him from his creative work but also caused him great mental anguish: "You cannot know, Titus, what a torture I find the three days preceding a concert." His music now became well known through the efforts of a number of first-rate performers: Clara Wieck, Liszt, Hiller, Kalkbrenner. Chopin was not like Liszt, that golden and gregarious Magyar who never tired of performing: "I wasn't meant to give concerts, but you are, by nature, because if you can't captivate your audience you can dominate it." Success brought out Chopin's patrician side. "His manners were so naturally aristocratic that he was instinctively treated like a prince," Liszt reported. His taste for luxury dictated that he keep a carriage, and that he wear white glacé gloves and a redingote tailored by Dautremont. All the money he earned went into the purchase of Louis XVI furniture for his new apartment in the Chaussée d'Antin (which his friends were already alluding to as Olympus), and into his charge accounts at Chardin the perfumer, Rapp the fashionable bootmaker, and Feideau the hatter. He countered Bohemian untidiness with dandyism, his fastidiousness being in particularly sharp contrast with the romantics whom he saw at the Café des Anglais and the Café de Paris. He was constantly being solicited for contributions to Polish exiles: "It would be unseemly for you to give less than 40,000 francs, but you can give more. . . ." Here was one genius who was not poverty-stricken, unlike Schubert, for example, who was not always able to scrape together a meal. But his friend Orlowski observed: "Chopin is turning all the ladies' heads and making the men jealous; he has become the fashion. But he is consumed by homesickness."

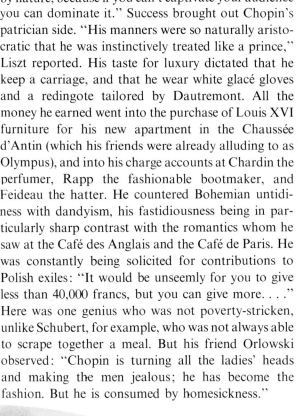

Above: Boulevard Poissonière, as painted by Dagnan. Chopin lived here, at No. 27, when he first came to Paris. Opposite page: An allegory, in the taste of the period, which celebrates the triumphs of Bellini and the singer M. Felicita Garcia, known as La Malibran (1808-1836, first portrait); Chopin, too, considered her second only to Giuditta Pasta (third portrait). Between the two is Luigi Cherubini, who was then the director of the Paris Conservatory; Paer, the conductor of the court orchestra, introduced Chopin to him, and also to Rossini (last portrait), director of the Italian theatre.

A BEAUTIFUL
COUNTESS

Chopin's first love in Paris was Delphine Potocka, about whom Krasinski was to write, ". . . you are Beauty itself." The beautiful countess lived alone. She had an income of 100,000 francs, a rapidly changing roster of admirers—among them the Duc d'Orléans and the Duc de Montfort—and great musical talent: she sang beautifully and played the piano. One evening she asked Chopin to "interpret her" through the piano; so he stretched her shawl on the keyboard and improvised, as if to say "you have no secrets from me." It was to be a satisfying relationship. Chopin was young and sure of himself; he was a match for the famous beauty. Delphine's life had not been a happy one; five of her children had died, and she had a difficult husband from whom she was separated. Chopin admired her unconquerable spirit. He wrote her that Liszt as a composer "is a brilliant anthologist who, in variously coloured bindings, collects the works of others."

The news of Costantia's marriage did not disturb him ("That does not harm platonic affections," he wrote Titus); and in 1836, when "Costantia's" Concerto in F Minor was published, he re-

dedicated it to Delphine. Eventually, Delphine settled down with Krasinski, the poet of the *Not Divine Comedy*. But for the moment she was the Muse of the Olympus at 5, Chaussée d'Antin, where Chopin lived, and which had become the meeting place of the most prominent Poles in Paris. Among these were a number of great poets: Niemcewicz, Zaleski, Witwicki, and Mickiewicz, who towered above them all. Chopin's drawing room was often fragrant with the scent of violets. Silence would fall upon the guests when Liszt played the Etudes, Op. 10 (which Chopin had dedicated to him); or when Berlioz spoke of his new method of orchestration. In a contemporary cartoon he was shown conducting an orchestra of hissing snakes. And the appearance in Chopin's apartment of his old friend Dr. Jan Matuszinski created the illusion that they were all once more living in their happy world of Warsaw before the uprising. Chopin was not without detractors; there was the spiteful German critic, Rellstabb, and Field, an Irish pianist, the inventor of a new form of nocturne, who said that Chopin had a "sick-room talent".

Left: Bivouac of Russian troops on the Champs Elysées at the time of the Restoration. Opposite page: A painting by Leconte of the battle at the Porte St. Denis in July 1830. During that year, revolution spread all over Europe, from Poland to Belgium, the people and the bourgeoisie, disillusioned by the reactionary Bourbon restoration after Waterloo, rose up in arms. Their leaders were Thiers, the banker Lafitte and the irrepressible Lafayette. Charles X was forced into exile and the crown was offered to Louis-Philippe d'Orléans (the son of Philippe Egalité) shown (below) leaving Versailles with his sons in a painting by Vernet.

LIFE AMONG THE EXILES

In 1833, a pianist named Thalberg began to catch the public's attention. All Paris eagerly took sides in his rivalry with Liszt. Heine finally settled the matter by saying: "There is only one man I should place above them: Chopin." The year 1835 was a happy one for Chopin: he now had three publishers, Wessel in England, Breitkopf and Hartel in Germany, Schlesinger in France. In August he joined his parents in Karlsbad. By pure chance they were able to spend three weeks together, happily catching up on lost time. On his way back to Paris, Chopin stopped in Dresden at the invitation of Countess Teresa Wodzinska. He had been at school with her sons, and one of them, Antonin, now lived in Paris. Chopin suddenly found himself in a Polish atmosphere; once more the past was recaptured. Everyone was cordial; "Freddie's little corner" was permanently reserved.

Maria, the 16-year-old daughter of the Wodzinskis, was a favourite; she played the piano, painted, and wrote poetry. She had been nicknamed the "dark-haired daughter of Europe" by Louis Napoleon in Geneva, where the Wodzinskis had held open house for a year. Her idyll with Chopin lasted for a year, under the close supervision of the worldly countess, who was flattered to play hostess to a genius in love. Chopin, as he was taking his leave, dedicated to Maria his Farewell Waltz. She wrote to him: "How can I not deplore that your name is not Chopinski? If it were, the French would be robbed of the glory of being your compatriots!"

The following year Chopin worked hard. (The *Warsaw Courier* had to deny rumours of his death.) He received a tremendous ovation at the Salle Erard in Paris. He published a great many works, among which the first Ballade (Op. 23) may have been inspired by Maria. In July he rushed off to Marienbad to see the Wodzinskis again. Invited to the court in Dresden, he astonished everyone by refusing to play for the King. He was busy summoning up the courage to ask for Maria's hand. The Countess, suffering from tooth trouble, gave her consent, and promised to speak to her husband. Meantime she begged Chopin to keep the engagement secret and to learn to look after his health. He was to take his cough medicine regularly, wear woollen socks, and go to bed early! Maria joined in the chorus: she would send him a pair of slippers embroidered by her.

The youthful Franz Liszt (far left), by Devéria. It is difficult to draw an accurate word portrait or to appraise the role of the vibrant Magyar musician in musical history. Without being an uncompromising innovator like Berlioz, or an ecstatic composer like Schubert, or an invincible spirit like Beethoven, or an individual like Chopin, or an anguished romantic like Schumann, or an innocent like Mendelssohn, Liszt lived out his romanticism impartially between art and life. An early example of a certain type of modern intellectual, he did not turn his back on any philosophic or artistic movement of the changing times in which he lived, be it the mysticism of Lamennais or the superhumanism of Nietzsche or of Wagner. He aroused the usual amount of fanaticism characteristic of any period. In this respect he was like Paganini. Next to him, the tenor Rubini, star of the Opera. Below these portraits, the Concert Hall of the Paris Conservatory. This page, below: The entrance to the Louvre, by Bouhot.

A ROMANCE
BURNS ITSELF OUT

Victoria, Queen of England,
and Albert, Prince Consort.
Left: A "farewell evening" at the
Royal Theatre of London. Above:
Waterloo Bridge and Somerset
House, a view of prosperous
and prudish Victorian London,
where Chopin spent some time
in 1837 to forget the breaking
off of his engagement to Maria
Wodzinska. "One can have a
moderately good time in London
if one doesn't stay too long.
There are extraordinary things:
Imposing toilets too narrow to
turn around in. And the English!
And the horses! And the palaces!
And the pomp, and the carriages!
Everything, from the soap to the
razors, is extraordinary . . ." wrote
Chopin to a friend. Right: Teresa
and Matthew Wodzinski, who very
nearly became his in-laws.

After a trip to Leipzig, where he played for Robert Schumann, Chopin, by then secretly engaged, found letters from the Wodzinskis waiting in Paris.

What was Maria Wodzinska to him? This somewhat doll-like child, who did not know how to love him, was to have an unhappy life. She was the embodiment of an ideal of aristocratic life, the mirror of childhood. The faces of Elise, Wanda and Costantia were superimposed upon hers. She might have provided the link with Poland that Chopin needed in Paris. This model child turned out to be only a second-rate Muse. She wrote to him no letters, being content to add postscripts to her family's: "We can't seem to console ourselves at your departure . . . then Mama had a tooth pulled. . . ." The mother's letters were more interesting. It was she who begged him "to keep the secret, and to stay well; everything will depend upon this."

This once-blazing love burned itself out tearfully in

a correspondence edited by Maria's mother. The Countess must have been persuaded by her husband that a match between their daughter and an artist, however famous, was unsuitable. Meanwhile, Chopin still thought himself engaged: "I am thinking of the slippers," he wrote, "and I play at twilight. . . ." He kept an eye on Antonin, lent him money, sent a piano to the Wodzinskis. But gradually letters from Sluzewo, the Wodzinski estate, became less frequent. Soon they ceased altogether.

Chopin had a bad winter in 1837; he was troubled by grippe, and even more by depression. Yet, he strove to forget his troubles. His reaction to the disappointment that scarred him for years is recorded by a friend, Kozmian: "Chopin is here in London with Pleyel, famous for his pianos and his wife's vivacity. They have come to have a good time, they stay in the best hotels, and are looking for opportunities to spend as much money as possible."

*Above: Contemporary print
showing a café on the
Pont Neuf in Paris during the
Restoration. After the passing
of the Napoleonic meteor
the Bourbons reclaimed
the French throne.
This did not prevent
the gentleman in the centre
of the print from wearing
the dashing Napoleonic cocked
hat. Right: Rummage sale
organized in the drawing room
of Princess Marcelline
Czartoryska in Paris in 1844.
Since the city was the
refuge of political exiles
from half of Europe,
sales like this one were
frequent. Chopin, rightly or
wrongly considered wealthy,
never failed to contribute
to events of this kind.*

"CANNON HIDDEN UNDER THE FLOWERS"

"Were the powerful tyrant from the North (Czar Nicholas I) to realize how hostile to him are Chopin's compositions, his simple mazurkas, he would forbid their performance: they are cannon hidden under the flowers," wrote Robert Schumann in a long article on Chopin's art. Although at first Chopin did not much appreciate the admiration of his German colleague, the two composers later met amicably. He also recognized in Clara Wieck a great interpreter of his compositions. She was the future "immortal beloved" of musical history, the wife of Robert Schumann, and loved by Brahms as well. As for the "tyrant from the North", in 1837 Chopin refused an invitation to become the Czar's court pianist, despite all the advantages such a position entailed: pensions and attendant honours. "Even though I did not physically take part in the Polish revolution of 1831, my soul participated in it, and I aspire to no other title than that of *émigré*," he replied.

The music that Chopin published after the termination of his ill-fated engagement to Maria Wodzinska marked the beginning of a new period both in his love life and in the development of his music. In the autumn of 1837, the Etudes, Op. 25, appeared, dedicated to the Countess d'Agoult, Liszt's tempestuous mistress; then the Impromptu Op. 29, the Mazurka Op. 30, the Scherzo in B Flat Minor, and the Nocturnes, Op. 32. In February, 1838, Chopin appeared at the Tuileries Palace before Louis Philippe and the court, who acclaimed him with wild enthusiasm. The only criticism levelled at him was that "he had made himself scarce." The *Musical World* referred to him as "the most reserved and the least vain of all pianists..." And Legouvé wrote in the *Gazette Musicale:* "Chopin reserves his great genius for an audience of five or six. However, today, in order to help a compatriot, he overcame his aversion to the public.... Let this triumph make up your mind ... don't persevere in your selfishness, and, when people ask: Who is the leading pianist, Liszt, Thalberg? the world will reply: Chopin." Even Paganini, the artist who in 1829 in Warsaw had seemed unsurpassable, came to pay his respects.

Chopin, presumably in 1835, for the water colour is by Maria Wodzinska, his erstwhile fiancée. Claudine Potocka (left), another philanthropic Polish lady living in a foreign land: she was known as "the angel of the émigrés". She died in Geneva in 1836. Below this, Vincenzo Bellini. Chopin met him in the winter of 1835 and became genuinely fond of the Sicilian, whose Norma was one of his favourite operas. Bellini's death, in the same year, was a great blow to him. The Italianate character of some of Chopin's works (the two concertos, a few Nocturnes, the fourth Scherzo) is reminiscent of the melodic quality of Bellini's music.

FIRST MEETING WITH GEORGE SAND

When Chopin thought he was still engaged to Maria Wodzinska, Mme Lenormand, a crystal-gazer, predicted a happy future for him. How could he not believe it? She had made the same prediction for Liszt and his Countess d'Agoult. And Marie and Franz were happy, one of the "couples of the century": a position attained by a combination of scandal and talent. Marie had left her husband and children, keeping only her title, to pursue, along with her great passion, an unexpected literary success (she wrote under the pseudonym of Daniel Stern). Liszt, four years her junior, was the sort of man who, with an eye out for posterity, wrote in a hotel register: "birthplace: Parnassus; residence: the land of doubt; destination: the truth." Marie aspired to the role of a patroness of the arts in the grand tradition. She made a cult of genius, and it would seem that she had marked Chopin for her own. Liszt and Marie shared a salon at the Hotel de France with George Sand, the well-known author of *Indiana*. Together they entertained Sue, Mickiewicz, Sainte-Beuve, Leroux, Chopin and Heine. Liszt, whose motto was *génie oblige,* had good reason for bringing Chopin, a disappointed suitor,

and George Sand together, for he was aware of Marie's interest in the young Pole. He brought George Sand to Chopin's apartment on a December evening in 1836. It was one of those evenings at Chopin's when Heine would tell legends about ancient Nordic lands, about frozen wastelands forever lost; and Chopin would improvise on the piano for hours on end. Finally he would run a finger along the keyboard in a lively *glissando* to dispel the mood and bring his listeners back to the present. "He passed through our lives like a spirit," Liszt wrote later. The Magyar eventually wrote an excellent biography of his friend.

That evening, George wore the Polish colours, crimson and white. She was being courted by Eugene Sue. She listened to Nourrit, the tenor, arbiter of elegance and art in Paris, a neurotic who soon committed suicide. She was silent when Liszt, an initiate in the mysticism and humanitarianism of Lamennais, held forth. Like her host, Chopin, she disliked the kind of drawing-room philosophy that was evolved between dessert and coffee. The following summer she waited in vain for Chopin, whom she had invited to her country house at Nohant. But she knew how to wait.

*Opposite page,
clockwise from top: Clara
Wieck, Robert Schumann's
wife. Next, her romanticist
husband who, he said, "had
learned music from the poetry
of Johann Paul (Richter)
rather than from essays on
counterpoint." His admiration
and affection for Chopin
were not reciprocated.
Below: Maria Wodzinska,
once beloved of Chopin;
next, Felix Mendelssohn.
In 1834 at Aix-la-Chapelle
(left) Mendelssohn pronounced
Chopin "a pianist without a
peer", but a little too "precious".
Above: Dresden in 1829; here
Chopin heard Goethe's Faust
set to the music of Spohr:
"A horrible but great fantasy"
was his comment.*

Below: George Sand and Casimir Dudevant, the famous writer and her husband, who was decidedly "not an aristocrat". Their marriage ended in divorce. George Sand was born Aurore Dupin jn Paris in 1804, daughter of Maurice and Sophie Dupin. At her birth, the music of a quadrille was being played in the next room. Chopin, too,

was born to music, in 1810; in his case, itinerant violinists were playing for alms in the frozen courtyard of Zelazowa Wola. And, like him, the authoress had Polish ancestors, the most notable one being Maurice de Saxe, the natural son of King Augustus II of Poland. She shared Chopin's life for nine years.

The authoress, who was then 34 years old, was one of the survivors of the "break-up of the century". She had known ecstasy with the poet Musset on their trip together to Italy. There had followed debts, quarrels, an end to the ecstasy, heartbreak and sickness for him, and finally rebirth for her in her house at Nohant—this after a crisis that had made her consider suicide.

George approached Chopin, six years her junior, with a caution unusual for her. What was this man, who seemed to be alive only when he played the piano for a few intimate friends; who was indifferent to the adoration that the public showed him; who was badly informed, so it seemed to her, on non-platonic love? Was this Chopin sentimentally available? George Sand wrote to Albert Grzymala, a mutual friend, a 5,000-word letter in which she exhorted him to sound out Chopin, to search his soul: "I must know how things stand. . . ." George Sand was very much the intellectual. This unusual letter laid bare a state of mind, and considered the prospect of a healing relationship. Could she love Chopin with the certainty the he would reciprocate? "He is afraid of people, he is afraid of who knows what. . . ."

Then she went on to assert the right of a person to reconstitute for himself or herself a spiritual virginity. In all her famous "brief encounters", including her marriage to the alcoholic Baron Dudevant, George Sand knew she had always been alone—as had her "Polish angel". And she knew she still had resources. So what promised to be a stormy alliance—inevitably, with two temperamental and creative personalities involved—could not help but appear to both parties a challenge too attractive to be ignored. During the summer of 1838 George Sand stayed in Paris—unusual for her—and in an attic of the Hotel de France wrote a new novel, *Spiridion*. Chopin did not leave the city either. George sent progress reports on the affair to a friend, Mme Marliani: "The sky is changeable; one week he says: 'Yes, no, but perhaps . . .'" Happiness came in the evening when they welcomed together those friends who had been the habitués of his drawing room.

Opposite page: The gallery of celebrities who gathered at George Sand's house in Nohant, a caricature by Maurice Dudevant, the writer's son. Among them can be recognized the painter Delacroix, Liszt, the actor Bocage, the painter Charpentier, the politician Arago, the engraver Calamatta. Above: The Waltz, a licentious print of slightly earlier date (Paris, Bibliothèque Nationale). Chopin's Waltzes did not conform to the Viennese spirit of Strauss; they indicate rather that the composer had in mind the lesson taught by von Weber, Schubert, Mozart himself. There was an ironic preciosity in encounters between the beautiful girls and the youthful Werthers who flitted about under the candelabra in the drawing rooms of the nobility. Could one dance to Chopin's Waltzes? "Yes, but only . . . countesses", wrote Schumann. Left: Hector Berlioz, who revolutionized orchestration. Next: Nicolo Paganini. Chopin heard the Genoese violinist for the first time in 1829, when Paganini was in Warsaw for the coronation of Czar Nicholas I, and was thunderstruck by his virtuosity. His Etudes show Paganini's influence.

MAJORCA—
AN IDYLL
TURNED SOUR

*The Chartreuse of
Valdemosa at Palma di
Majorca, in a sketch by
George Sand (above) and
as it appears today (right).
The writer and Chopin
lived there during their stay
in Palma in the autumn
and winter of 1838-39.*

"Here I am at Palma di Majorca, among palm trees, cedars, aloes, pomegranate trees, everything in its natural environment that the Jardin des Plantes has in its greenhouses. The sky is turquoise, the sea azure, the mountains emerald and the climate paradisiacal. There is sun all day long: everyone wears summer clothes. It is hot, and at night, for hours on end, guitars and singing can be heard. There are echoes of Africa everywhere. In short, an enchanted life," Chopin wrote to Jules Fontana from Majorca on November 15, 1838. To visit this shining Mediterranean isle, Chopin and George Sand incurred debts without a qualm: he to Pleyel, she to her publisher. It was George herself who planned the expedition. She had decided that the beginning of their romance deserved a special setting, outside city walls. Switzerland was ruled out as being too commonplace. Too many others had gone there: Liszt, Simon, the followers of Napoleon. To be a true romantic, one must travel. But this time something unprecedented was called for, perhaps something exotic: "The

Orient! the Orient, poets, what do you see there? Turn your eyes and your minds toward the Orient!" Victor Hugo wrote. Asia, Africa were already beckoning. Their friend Delacroix, the painter, had managed to get himself attached to a diplomatic mission in Algeria, to the benefit of his art. But trips of such length were not feasible with only publishers' advances to defray expenses; on the other hand, Majorca, jewel of the Mediterranean, exotic, almost unknown, accessible, and with an ideal climate, was just what was wanted. George Sand and Chopin left Paris separately, keeping their expedition secret except from their intimate friends, and joined forces in Perpignan. "Fresh as a rose" was George Sand's description of Chopin when they started out. They established themselves on the island with great satisfaction. The only inconveniences seemed to be the mail and the roads, which were quite hopeless. "And yet, dear Jules," Chopin wrote after a few days, "one couldn't find a single Englishman in the neighbourhood, not even a consul." But disaster struck. Hardly

had they settled in a villa when they had to move out, burning furniture behind them and whitewashing the walls as though they had been infected. The rainy season had descended on the island, a phenomenon for which they were unprepared. And although George and her children, whom she had brought with her, did not feel its effects at all, Chopin began to cough and to spit up blood. "From that moment we became an object of fear and horror," Chopin recounted. "Three doctors gathered for a consultation (odious and how different from Paris!): the first two opined I should die soon, the third considered me already dead." And so, made as unwelcome "as Mohammedans", and without a house, they found refuge in an ancient ruined convent—a place undeniably suggestive, whose exotic aura did not, however, make up for autumn rains. No carriage could reach it, which made provisioning difficult. The moods of Maria Antonia, the cook, were equally difficult. The ghost of a former bell ringer glided through the corridors, knocking at the doors

of the cells and calling the departed monks; his wild laughter echoed everywhere.

For Chopin, it was a nightmare. "You can shout yourself hoarse," he wrote, "only silence will answer." And George Sand agreed: "Never have I heard such wailing voices, such despairing howls as those the wind carries here." Nonetheless, the Pleyel piano came through customs—another exhausting procedure—and Chopin finished a ballade, a scherzo, the Preludes. Finally, money gave out: "I am leaving Majorca, making exorcisms, like a primitive," Sand was to say. "It is a diabolic country," Chopin wrote. A fitting epilogue to this soaking honeymoon was the return trip on the *El Mallorquin*, a miserable little tub. In the hold were pigs that were beaten at regular intervals to keep them from being seasick. It was no wonder that Chopin had a haemorrhage on the French warship to which George had him transferred as soon as they reached Barcelona.

*Below: The cell occupied by
Chopin at Valdemosa;
sketch of a country dance:
two drawings rapidly done
by George Sand at Majorca.
The writer collected
her travel notes
in a volume, published
in 1855, entitled*
A Winter in Majorca.

*Left: The Pleyel piano at
which Chopin composed his
music in Majorca. Purchased at
the time by a local banker,
it is now again at the
Charterhouse of Valdemosa.
Opposite page: The garden of
the cloisters as it is today and
as it appears in a water colour
in the museum in La Châtre.
The ink portrait of Chopin
(upper right), done by George
Sand, is at Nohant.*

VALLDEMOSA - MALLORCA

EVEN MASTERPIECES HAVE THEIR PRICE

There is something indisputably ironic in the fate that overtook this man who, on a Mediterranean island, suffered more from the weather than he ever had in his native northern climate. However, on the credit side, Chopin returned from Majorca with the Preludes finished (and already sold to Pleyel, from whom he had received an advance of 500 francs before leaving for his vacation). The Preludes were dated January, 1839. They are among the masterpieces of the romantic period. "Written, apparently, at one sitting, they have the fast-winged pace of a work of genius," Liszt wrote. Perfect in their brevity, they are pure Chopin. They reveal the whole gamut of his creative genius, his ability to convey the happiness and sorrow of life, to capture a moment of joy or grief. His Slavic soul is glimpsed in fragments of infernal melody without relief or hope. Some of the Preludes are solemn, majestic, grandiloquent; others are gently melodic or elegiac. Technically, 24 Preludes are set out according to the 24 keys in the normal scale, whereby each major key is followed by its relative minor key—C major followed by A minor, G major by E minor, etc. In

*Adolphe Nourrit (far left).
The famous tenor committed suicide
at 37 in Naples after giving what he
considered a poor performance of
Norma. He was afraid he had lost
his voice. Meyerbeer, Rossini,
Halvéy and Aubèr had written for
him. Chopin played at his funeral
service in Marseilles (March, 1839).
Jules Fontana (next to him), a*

*mediocre but most devoted colleague
of Chopin's, also committed suicide,
in 1869. "Marseilles is an old but
not ancient city, and very noisy.
Next month we'll set out from here
for Nohant; there I shall kiss you but
without my moustache. I wonder if
yours has suffered the same fate as
mine?" Chopin wrote to his friend
Grzymala in March, 1839. Centre:*

*The port of Marseilles in an old
print. Below, and opposite: two
lithographs of rural scenes that
appeared in* The Friend of the People
*in Warsaw. Scenes like this were
a common sight to the young
Chopin when he was vacationing in
the Polish countryside. He never
forgot them, and brought them to
life again in his mazurkas.*

terms of feeling, they are a real *tour de force,* made possible by his self-knowledge. Schumann wrote, "He is here recognizable even in the pauses and the silences."

Even masterpieces have their price; but the artist and the "merchants" made very different valuations of these when they came on the market. Jules Fontana, the factotum friend in Paris who was forever tangling with Chopin's publishers, received from the composer, still in Marseilles, a letter dated March 12, 1839: "So Pleyel thinks my manuscripts too expensive! If I have to sell them cheap, I prefer to sell them to Schlesinger, who adores me, I suppose, because he manages to rob me! Don't send any manuscripts until you have the cash in hand! Lord, what a fate to be forever obliged to deal with that riffraff. . . . And Probst, who wants to pay me 300 francs for a mazurka, is a highway robber; for the last ones I had no trouble getting 800 francs. I prefer to give them away for nothing, as I did once, rather than to have to deal with those idiots. If you are planning to become a shoemaker, don't supply shoes to either Pleyel or Probst: let them go barefoot! . . ."

THE PERFECTIONIST

"You are not tubercular; all you have is a chronic inflammation of the larynx; I see no reason to be frightened," assured Dr. Papet, the first guest at Nohant after the ill-fated idyll. Chopin asked nothing better than to believe this diagnosis. After Majorca, George's château meant recovery for Chopin. Surrounded by friends, he began to get better. He prepared a pantomime for the little theatre at Nohant. He gave lessons to George's daughter Solange, to whom he was devoted. He avoided billiards, which appealed to the other guests: Grzymala; Emanuel Arago, a politician; Marie Dorval, the Comédie Française actress whose assidiousness in the past had caused George Sand to be known as a modern-day Sappho. And he worked. He corrected the Paris edition of Bach: "I don't pretend to know Bach better than others do, but I am convinced that I understand him." He finished the Sonata in B Minor, Op. 35; the third Scherzo, Op. 39; the Impromptu in F Sharp Major. After a day of work, it was to George that Chopin turned: "He consults me as Molière used to consult his servant girl," said George with wry humour. She was an excellent listener. An efficient and tireless worker who could write in the morning a manuscript she had planned during the night, she was witness to Chopin's creative torment—"a perfectionist". He shut himself in his room for days on end, wept, rewrote the same measure a hundred times. Then he would start again, yet often the final composition was identical with the first draft. George finally lost her patience. Chopin was no longer a great passion; he was rather like a third child, to be looked after and protected. Also, having partially recovered his health, he tried diverting himself with a neighbourhood beauty. At last, taking stock of their future, the couple decided to go to Paris, taking separate apartments to allow each of them reasonable freedom of action. The immediate result was a great deal of work for the ever-obliging Fontana: "Find two apartments next to each other," Chopin wrote to him. "Please also see to the wallpaper, which is to be dove-grey with a dark-green border." There was also to be a red sofa and some frilled grey curtains in the latest fashion by Dautremont.

Opposite page: Chopin, in a portrait by Scheffer. Below: Two caricatures by Maurice, George Sand's son: Sand going off into ecstasy as she listens to the prodigious Liszt; and Sand with Balzac (author of The Human Comedy), *moustached, swathed in his robe, watching a performance of the puppet theatre at Nohant.*

Left: Aurore Dupin, in a portrait by Charpentier. Her first story, written in collaboration with her friend Jules Sandeau for the Revue de Paris, *was signed Jules Sand. Later, she wrote the novel* Indiana *alone at Nohant. It was the editor Latouche who fixed her pseudonym: "Today it is S. George; let the lady add the last name Sand to George, and we'll know where we stand!"*

THE NEW WAVE

In October, 1839, Chopin and George Sand were once more settled in Paris, the musician at 5 Rue Tronchet, the writer at 16 Rue Pigalle. From Nohant Chopin had sent the following instructions to Fontana: "Arrange things, dearest friend, so that sad thoughts will be kept at bay and so that coughing will not suffocate me. Wish me better health; I should be grateful if you could make yourself younger, and if you could arrange things so that we might never have been born. . . ."

On October 29, Chopin played at Saint-Cloud for Louis Philippe. Ignaz Moscheles, the German virtuoso who performed that same evening and who once had described the Études as "unplayable break-finger exercises", tonight shared the King's opinion: "Chopin is unique in the world of pianists." Despite this, Chopin was not content. In order to re-create the illusion of family life, he took a studio in the Rue Pigalle, but he soon spent more and more time next door, at No. 16. Here, George Sand, who was always in touch with new political and social trends, gathered a group of people committed to the "new wave": Louis Blanc, historian and social democrat; the Republican Cavaignac; Pierre Leroux, the standard-bearer of a new kind of social Christianity and of a "truth constantly marching forward which goes from nation to nation; at the moment it is embodied in Poland, whence it will spread throughout the world." Sand was among those who, according to Balzac, were "steeped in Poland". At this time she published an essay on Byron, Goethe and Mickiewicz. Chopin found in Delacroix his patron saint. The great painter considered Chopin second only to Mozart, who was the musical idol of both of them. Chopin, on the other hand, preferred Ingres to Delacroix. Each of them, an innovator in his own art, preferred the classics. They had in common consumption, asceticism and that "moderate kindness" which—according to Baudelaire, a friend of the painter—"is always inseparable from genius."

Honoré de Balzac (below, left), a writer who rather irritated Chopin. Balzac wrote of George Sand in 1838: "I found my colleague, Sand, wrapped in a dressing gown, smoking an after-dinner cigar. She wore pretty yellow slippers, charming stockings, red pantaloons." Next, Alfred de Musset, "Miss Byron", as Sainte-Beuve nicknamed him because of his delicate charm. The poet wrote to George Sand in July 1833: "I must confess, Madame, to something foolish and absurd: I love you, Madame, I love you as though I were a child!" His "affectionate friendship" with the authoress later created quite a stir. The last is Adam Mickiewicz (1798–1855), one of the greatest romantic poets, the messiah of the rebirth of nations through freedom. Another Polish poet, Krasinski, wrote of him: "He is the twinkling light of national poetry, his works are as immense as the ages, as the Pyramids in the desert, the granite nucleus of our literature." Mickiewicz never forgave Chopin for not having given Poland a great national work. Opposite page: George Sand's passion for politics gave scope to cartoonists. The authoress is shown with Ledru-Rollin. Above: Paris in the mid-1840's: the Place de la Concorde.

A TRIUMPH AT 6,000 FRANCS

For Chopin, the year 1840 marked the beginning of an intense period of creativity. For Sand, it marked a theatrical fiasco, *Cosima*. Her heroine bore the name of the daughter of Liszt and Marie d'Agoult, the Cosima who later became Richard Wagner's wife. Mme d'Agoult thoroughly enjoyed her famous colleague's fiasco. She now hated the couple whose fame had overshadowed her own romance with Liszt, and she had dubbed Chopin "an ostrich powdered with sugar".

Chopin had a reciprocal grudge against Liszt. The Hungarian had used the fastidious Chopin's apartment for an assignation with Mme Pleyel and had not bothered to clear away the traces afterwards. But the gentlemen forgave more readily than the ladies. Indeed, when in April 1841 the gilded youth, the bluestockings, the financial world, the aristocracy and the greatest intellects of Paris crowded the Salle Pleyel to hear Chopin play, Liszt wrote a glowing review for the *Gazette Musicale*. The critics agreed unanimously. The triumph was worth 6,000 francs: "Try reading your poetry to an audience for 40 minutes and you will see if you will be paid an equal amount," was the comment of the poet Witwicki, who, 10 years earlier, had urged Chopin to stay out of the Polish revolution of 1831, serving his country by his art instead.

Mickiewicz, on the other hand, was increasingly hostile to Chopin. The poet and the composer were destined to pass each other like enemy ships in the night, in the sea of Parisian society. They seldom met. In 1840, Mickiewicz obtained the chair of Slavic Literature at the Collège de France. And, having made Slavicism the topic of the day, he officiated as national prophet. Michelet, Sainte-Beuve, Montalembert and Lamartine attended his lectures, as did George Sand, who often took her place beside him amid great applause. Mickiewicz preached agreement between nations; he was indifferent to crowned heads. He also wrote for the newspapers. Sand summed him up as a combination of Joan of Arc and Socrates. Mickiewicz called Chopin "Sand's black spirit", and disapproved of his "glittering social life." Still, one of Chopin's ballades was inspired by a poem of Mickiewicz, *Switez*.

"THE ILLUSION OF THE GOOD PROVINCIAL NEIGHBOUR"

Nohant in 1841: Chopin was working on the Tarantelle ("I hope it will be a long time before I write anything worse"); the third Ballade, Op. 47, in which the voices of ancient Slavic legends are mingled with other echoes; the Polonaise, Op. 44; and the Fantaisie in F Minor, masterpieces inspired by his native land. He discovered in himself a certain talent for snubbing busybodies, even when they were friends of George's: "la Rosières, that unbearable creature who somehow managed to find her way into my garden, and nibbles and looks for truffles among the roses. . . ." The unfortunate woman no doubt deserved this, for she had taken it upon herself to send a portrait of Chopin—as a wedding present—to Maria Wodzinska, who was marrying Count Skarbek of Zelazowa Wola. But he struck up a friendship with the season's guest of honour, the fascinating Pauline Viardot Garcia, who was almost as well known as her sister, La Malibran. Pauline was later to marry the novelist Turgenev, her second husband. It is to her we owe the transcriptions for voice of some of Chopin's Mazurkas.

During the following winter, Chopin had another triumph at the Salle Pleyel. (Mme Viardot Garcia appeared on the same programme.) On the same freezing February night, his old teacher Zywny died in Warsaw. Then, in April, Jan Matuszynski, the faithful friend who shared Chopin's apartment and his consumption, also died. Chopin felt the blow with alarming force. It created a gap which was filled only by the revival of his fears that he himself harboured the disease. Once more it was George Sand who saved him, rushing him to Nohant, where he was surrounded by friends. Among them was Delacroix, also ill. At Nohant, in 1842, Chopin wrote the 4th Ballade, Op. 52; the Scherzo, Op. 54; the Polonaise in A Flat Major, his greatest polonaise. The creative effort exhausted him to such a point that Sand had to keep her eye on him constantly. In the autumn they moved to two apartments at Numbers 5 and 9, Square d'Orléans, the "little Athens" of the city. Kalkbrenner, Dumas *père* and a few other friends also lived there. "Let us recreate, in this sad Paris," said Sand, "the illusion of the good provincial neighbour".

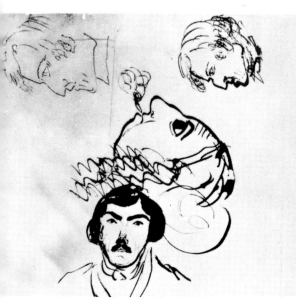

Above: Fan painted by Charpentier (who specialized in battle scenes), showing a gallery of the habitués of Nohant: from the left, the painter Calamatta (snake); Maurice Sand (four-legged sylph); Emmanuel Arago (a politician, shown here as Triton); Albert Grzymala, a friend; the actor Bocage (as a faun); Liszt on his knees before Sand, who holds a bird with Chopin's profile. Then, Delacroix as a shepherd; Féicien Malefille, trusted tutor at Nohant; Solange, George Sand's daughter, as a lion; the lawyer de Bourges, a skilled divorce specialist.

And last, Charpentier. Lower left: Delacroix, self-portrait; he was a great admirer of Chopin's, a frequent guest at Nohant. "You are a famous dauber," Sand wrote to him in 1838, after having admired his 'splendid, harrowing' Medea, "and, to persuade you to accept my invitation, I shall tell you that Chopin plays for our circle of friends with his elbows practically on the keyboard and that he is, in those moments, truly sublime." Next, Maciej Kamienski, Polish opera singer. This page: Caricatures of George Sand, Chopin and Delacroix, by George.

DOMESTIC PLEASURES AND QUARRELS

The year 1844 marked the high point for Chopin of life at Nohant. He held the centre of the stage. In the spring, his father died. In order to dispel the depression of her "sad angel", George invited Louise and Calasanzio Jedrzejewicz to Nohant. And so, after 14 years of separation, Chopin was reunited with his sister and brother-in-law. The reunion worked better than any medicine. Chopin began to work again, doing a rough draft of a third sonata, Op. 58, He noted with pride that his sister, an aspiring writer, exchanged views with George on the latter's new novel, *La Mare au Diable.*

Sand herself read it to her guests. It seemed to Chopin he couldn't ask for more. For one summer he had the pleasure of seeing "his two families" together. Never had his relations with George seemed so relaxed. Life was almost too peaceful: trouble must be brewing. The storm, as in any ordinary family, broke over the children, Solange and Maurice. Solange, beautiful,

restless (and malicious, added her mother), had no complaints about Chopin. Maurice, on the other hand, did not conceal his dislike and jealousy of his mother's friend, whose interference was "unwelcome and abusive". George found herself taking sides with her son. Tension grew daily. The first casualty was Jan, Chopin's new Polish servant, the victim of the pranks of Maurice and his cousin Augustine Brault. Chopin had never liked Augustine because he was afraid she would displace Solange in her mother's affections. The squabbles overflowed from the kitchen into the drawing room. Chopin took the complaints about Jan personally. He finally dismissed the valet. But dissension had reared its ugly head; charges and countercharges flew in the Square d'Orléans. Chopin sought support from his favourite, Solange, who like him was forever quarrelling with the arrogant Maurice. Sand took a dim view of the friendship between "her invalid" and her 16-year-old daughter.

Opposite page, above: Maurice and Solange, George Sand's children (born in 1823 and 1829) from her marriage to Baron Casimir Dudevant. "A weak lover, a mere shadow at Nohant, where George Sand's children accepted no guidance from him," the poet Benn wrote, in 1848, about Chopin in the second stanza of his biography in verse. Actually, the last verse refers to Maurice, who never could stand Chopin. Solange, on the other hand (below, in a caricature by Musset), was his favourite, and returned his affection. She disappointed him by marrying the sculptor Clésinger. It was even said that Chopin had asked for her hand.

Opposite page: The farm at Nohant in Berry, as it looks today. This farm provided many of the necessities for George Sand's household, which was always full of guests. An incurable "countrywoman", she took refuge there whenever she could. She had inherited it from her paternal grandmother, at Christmas in 1821; she was then 17. Above: The grounds of Nohant, as seen from the windows of the room occupied by Chopin. Upper left: Portrait of George Sand in 1838 by Delacroix. Below this, Liszt, Mme d'Agoult and a friend immersed in a philosophical discussion. The caricature, done by Sand, may have bèen done in 1837, when they were guests at Nohant.

"THE VICTIM" OF A LITERARY PORTRAIT

George Sand (above), dressed as a student. She had received a first-rate education at Nohant from her tutors: she had learned Latin and Greek, and had the use of a well-stocked library (Homer, Tasso and Racine were her favourite authors). She had learned to play the harpsichord and taken a course in anatomy. Her paternal grandmother, in whose charge she was, had hurriedly withdrawn her, after a brief stay, from a fashionable English Convent, since the girl, after a religious crisis, was threatening to take the veil. She took to wearing trousers in order to save on clothes during her first years in Paris when she lived, happy and poor, with Jules Sandeau. Right, drawing of her by Alfred de Musset.

On June 25, 1846, the *Courrier Français* carried the first instalment of a new novel by George Sand that was destined to have a quick financial success, *Lucrezia Floriani.* George Sand always took her characters from real life: *Elle et Lui* was based on her romance with Musset, and in *Consuelo,* the heroine was modelled after Mme Viardot Garcia, the famous singer. This time everyone in Paris was convinced that the two protagonists of the new novel, Karol (the slender, sickly prince who "does not see the ground, only the sky"), and the heroine, Lucrezia ("a widow with many lovers", six years older than her friend), could not be anyone except Chopin and the writer herself. Everyone sympathized with Chopin, "the victim".

It would be unfair to say that Karol, that difficult aesthete, is a negative character. But, undeniably, a fairly explicit spirit of accusation is present throughout the novel. From the standpoint of modern psychology, the novel might be viewed as a more or less conscious attempt to get rid of Chopin. George's major complaint seems to have been that, after eight years of life in common, Chopin still seemed to hold her at arm's length. Having permitted her to share his daily routine—meals, medicines—he had always denied her access to his inner life, drawing a veil over his own concept of life and, what was even more serious, his art. Sand, an intellectual, could not help being particularly resentful of this affront. What explanation could there be for this inaccessibility? Did Chopin ever really love her? This was obviously the question George-Lucrezia was asking herself. Did he not want her to know the answer? Had she let herself be taken in at the beginning? And was this incomplete partnership enough for a woman like Sand? In the novel, this lack of communication on the part of Karol kills Lucrezia. In life also, the more vulnerable of the two was to give way: only the roles were reversed.

Above: The little theatre of Nohant, where the guests sometimes doubled as audience and actors. Maurice Sand, who was studying painting with Delacroix, designed the sets; Chopin was one of the most reliable members of this troupe. The actor Piasecki, seeing Chopin act when the latter was still a schoolboy at the Lyceum, tried to persuade him to give up music for the stage. And Hervé, an actor in the French troupe in Warsaw, sang his praises when the young musician took a part in his repertory—his imitation of a tailor at work was particularly good. Left: Discussion at Nohant about the running of the theatre.

55

FAREWELL
TO NOHANT

In the *Story of My Life,* George Sand states that Chopin knew the contents of *Lucrezia Floriani* before its publication. In fact, he was in the habit of looking over her manuscripts. And it would seem that Solange also told him: "See, Mama has put you, too, in her new novel." George Sand, in order to counteract the unpopularity that all this brought her, hastily denied the Karol-Chopin identification. She even maintained that if he ever did make parallels, it was only as a result of gossip. This was an artless bit of cunning, which was certainly not typical of her. Chopin must certainly have understood at once the implications in *Lucrezia Floriani.* But he said nothing. His reaction was in keeping with Lucrezia-George's assertion: "Of all the reprisals, was not the most cruel one that he never gave up his frigid politeness?" This attitude must have increased George's irritation. Chopin was to speak only in passing of the novel, the following year, when he wrote to his sister Louise: "A work that has been less well received than her preceding ones..."

If Lucrezia's complaint was non-communication, George's was more specific: "Chopin's friendship has never been a refuge for me; all my strength came from my son." This Chopin could believe. Maurice was now master at Nohant. Work was exhausting for Chopin during the summer of 1846. He worked only intermittently on the Barcarolle, Op. 60.

He reacted to the hostile atmosphere by isolating himself. "I am so tired and so cheerless that I affect the young, and when I am present they enjoy themselves less." It is quite likely that Chopin, ill, nervous, and increasingly touchy, made his presence a burden. The climax came, as in any good middle-class family, at the dinner table. As Maurice helped himself to the choicest morsel of chicken, Chopin burst out: "I won't put up with condescension." Maurice decided that there was not room for both of them at Nohant. The incident was somehow pushed into the background, but when it came time to return to Paris, George did not accompany Chopin: she would spend the winter at Nohant. Chopin left, alone. This was November 10, 1846. He was never to return. From the cold city of Paris, he continued to write George cold, polite letters, precisely like those Prince Karol might have written.

"I have just come back from the Italian Theatre: I saw Jenny Lind (lower left) and the Queen. Both made a great impression. So did old Wellington. He was sitting under the royal box like a 'monarchic' old dog in his kennel. Then I met Jenny Lind who had saved a place for me: this Swedish lady does not glow with ordinary light, there is something of the aurora borealis about her," Chopin wrote from London on May 11, 1848, to his friend Grzymala. Next, the actor Bocage, a celebrity in Paris, and Marie Dorval (dressed as Marion Delorme), the actress who set hearts beating from the Boulevard du Crime to the Comédie Francaise. Upper left: Alexandre Dumas Senior (caricature by Musset). The Dumases, who in 1851 happened to acquire part of the Sand-Chopin correspondence, gave the letters back to the writer, who destroyed them. Next is Marie d'Agoult, Liszt's inspiration. Below: The rue de Castiglione in Paris, in a painting by Canella.

Above: The Boulevard des Capucines in a painting by Stanley at the Musée Carnavalet. Right: A barouche filled with costumed revellers in Paris. Opposite page, above: Louis Blanc, lithograph by Gattier, and Sainte-Beuve, drawn by Heim. Louis Blanc (1811-1882), a socialist, member of the revolutionary government of 1848, was a friend of George Sand. Sainte-Beuve (1804-1869), author of the Causeries du Lundi, *"was the father of modern criticism in France,"* Taine wrote. "His theory was that in order to evaluate the work of a writer, one must first know his life, the atmosphere in which he was formed, his friends, even the state of his health. He laid the foundation of what has been called the natural history of the mind, which likens the blossoming of genius to that of a plant. In this way, criticism is committed to the discovery of more than a moral truth or a literary ideal—to a historical scientific truth. There are bewildering biographies of the spirit among his works." He was a trusted friend of Sand's and the "director of her literary conscience", as Chopin put it. Below these two portraits: the Bolshoi Theatre in Moscow in a contemporary print. Czar Nicholas I invited Chopin to become court pianist, but the great Polish musician refused: he preferred remaining an émigré in Paris to giving pleasure with his music to those who, in 1831, had bloodily repressed the revolt of Warsaw.*

58

"AT LAST MY EYES ARE OPEN"

When George Sand reappeared in Paris in the spring of 1847, something between her and Chopin that had appeared dead seemed to come to life again. She seemed in excellent spirits; after considering various ways to marry off Solange, she had the satisfaction of promising her restless daughter's hand to a worthy young man, a member of the landed gentry, who had fallen in love at first sight. But an unexpected character appeared on the scene: Jean Clésinger, 33 years old, an athletic if somewhat limited sculptor—Chopin immediately dubbed him the "cuirassier". This "handsome devil", while he was doing a portrait of Solange ("the grand duchess"), wooed and speedily seduced her. George and her daughter retired to the country, using Chopin's carriage for the journey. Clésinger did not strike Chopin as being a desirable suitor, and he did not hesitate to point this out to George; she, on the other hand, was enthusiastic. This romantic substitution of a Michelangelo for a landed proprietor was bound to appeal to her. Chopin, who had not been invited to the wedding at Nohant, and who was recovering from a severe attack of asthma, sent his best wishes. It was soon evident that Chopin had correctly sized up the situation. George never forgave him for being right. Clésinger proved to be a violent man, good only at incurring debts. One evening a quarrel broke out. Clésinger, mallet in hand, lunged at Maurice, and struck George Sand. She threw the newlyweds out. Solange, who was expecting a baby, wanted to use Chopin's carriage, which her mother had kept at Nohant. George refused. Solange then appealed directly to Chopin, in Paris, who had no choice but to answer that it was at her disposal. George lost no time in seizing the pretext. She wrote to Chopin, urging him to break off with the Clésingers, but Chopin promised nothing. This was the last straw for Sand. She wrote to a friend: "The Clésingers and Chopin, who is supposed to be my most devoted friend: Splendid! . . . I know what Chopin's miserable little mind is capable of when it's a matter of credulity. But at last my eyes are open, and I shall never again allow my flesh and blood to be a pasture for ingratitude and perversity."

59

The year 1848, a great revolutionary time in Europe. On February 22, 1848, the people of Paris were again in arms on the streets. They went to Versailles. They demanded reforms. They sang the Marseillaise. Louis Philippe, King of the French, fled to Saint-Cloud (print below). He reached England incognito as Mr. Smith.

THE LAST PAINFUL MEETING

Centre: The sack of the Tuileries, another episode of the Revolution of 1848 in Paris, shown in a contemporary print bearing the inscription: "Respect Christ, for he is your master." Above: Polish exiles leaving France to return home: Poland also was up in arms against Russia. Right: The Parisian mob invading the Tuileries.

"Friends came this morning to tell me that I ought to give a concert and not think of anything except to sit at the piano and play. The concert has been sold out for a week. The public is making plans for a second one I haven't even thought of as yet. The Court wanted forty tickets; all this expectation fills me with wonder. I must practise a little to quiet my conscience, because it seems to me I have never played so badly as now. Pleyel jokes about my stupidity and, to encourage me, promises to fill the room with flowers. It shall be as though I were at home and my eyes will see only familiar faces."

After the rupture with George Sand, in August, 1847, Chopin never stopped trying to re-create a life for himself. He went to the country with the Rothschilds, succumbed to what he described as a vile grippe, prepared for a concert. But his efforts were only half-hearted. He sent to the publisher, Breitkopf, three Waltzes Op. 64, three Mazurkas Op. 63, and the Sonata for Cello—the last compositions to appear while he was still alive. Around him the vacuum grew. Witwicki died. "And I? I shall end up by believing myself immortal," he had said with bitter irony when the 15-year-old Filchst died, the promising pupil for whom Liszt had prophesied a great future. As for George, she sent Chopin one last letter, which Delacroix refers to in his *Journal:* "A horrible letter in which cruel passions and long-repressed impatience come to the surface in a contrast that would be interesting if it were not this particular case." And she continued to make excuses for herself. "Since the Clésingers and Chopin will continue to blow the trumpets against us," she admonished Maurice, "you, too, must blow the truth in Mme Marliani's (ears). . . ." But this year, 1847, had been a bad one for her also. "Without Maurice," she was to confess later, "I should have taken my life."

And it was at the door of Mme Marliani, with whom they had enjoyed their best meals, that George Sand and Chopin met casually one last time in March, 1848. A little girl had been born to Solange; it was Chopin who announced the event to George Sand. "How are you?" "Well." That was all. They were never to see each other again.

THE HOUR OF
REVOLUTION

On February 12, 1848, "tout Paris" came to the Salle Pleyel for what turned out to be Chopin's last concert in France. Chopin, who had not appeared on the concert stage for six years, played as he had never played before. It was as though he knew that he was celebrating not only his own apotheosis but also that of an entire society. The repeat performance never took place. On February 22, the Marseillaise was heard once more in the streets of Paris; once more the *garde nationale* went over to the side of the people. Revolution, the recurring motif in the life of Chopin, coincided this time with a crucial turning point in his life. Power passed into the hands of George Sand's friends of the new wave, among them Louis Blanc and Arago. Malefille, the former tutor at Nohant, became the director of Versailles. The King and "tout Paris" quickly crossed the Channel.

With Louis Philippe gone, it was not only France that continued to be restless. As in 1831, the spirit of revolution was abroad throughout Europe. Some of its leaders were romantic poets, like Lamartine, the new head of the republican government. "We ask for news, as did the ancient Athenians, and the cannon booms its answer," said Zaleski. Poland, in 1846, had fired the opening salvo of the Revolution, and already many of her sons lay dead. The Polish struggle had struck chords of sympathy in France. The railroads gave free transportation up to the frontiers to volunteers on their way to Poznan, where Mieroslawski was putting together an army.

In Italy, Mickiewicz was forming another "Polish Legion". Like other exiles, Chopin lived through days of hope, despair and enthusiasm. For a fleeting moment he could again believe in his hope for the rebirth of Poland. "My compatriots are meeting in Poznan," he wrote to Fontana in April. "As a start, Czartoryski has gone.... Now everything reeks of war. The Italians have started. Milan has thrown out the Austrians.... The French will doubtless send reinforcements. The Muscovites will certainly run into trouble when they march against the Prussians.... This will not occur without terrible events, but at the end of all this there will be a splendid, a great Poland."

Above: The celebration at the proclamation of the Second Republic in Paris (February 24, 1848): Delacroix wrote about it: "The ox Apis, allegorical triumphal carts followed by 400 virgins: it took a revolution to produce so many marvels!" The head of the government, which was formed with the help of the socialist Ledru-Rollin, was Lamartine (on horseback, in print below), the author of Meditations. *Many of George Sand's friends came to power: Pierre Leroux, a philosopher and pamphleteer, who founded in 1839 with George Sand the* Revue Indépendante; *Arago and Louis Blanc, who inspired the labour movement and founded the national workshops; Malefille, former tutor at Nohant. Sand took a great deal of trouble to find posts for her friends. She also took an active part in politics, and had Maurice elected mayor of Nohant. Opposite page, above: Presentation to the National Assembly of a petition for Poland in revolt against Russia. Polish legions had been formed by Mickiewicz in Italy, by Chopin's friend Szulezewski in Turkey, by Mieroslawski in Poznan. Opposite page, below: A meeting of the Assembly of 1848.*

A WARM WELCOME IN LONDON

Chopin arrived in London on April 21, 1848. Jane Stirling, who had arranged his London expedition, settled him in a cosy apartment on Bentinck Street that was even stocked with writing paper bearing his initials. This and other exquisite courtesies soon caused Chopin to move to 48 Dover Street; already there were too many rumours of an absurd marriage with this heiress who aspired to the role of George Sand II without being suited to the part. She was too attentive, too rich; she hadn't enough temperament.

Crossing the Channel was madness, in view of the smog and Chopin's health, but he wanted to break away from Paris after George Sand's defection, and he needed to give concerts to replenish his funds. A real Parisian season was in full swing in London. There, Chopin found Kalkbrenner, Osborne, Thalberg and Mme Viardot Garcia, who sang some of his Mazurkas at Covent Garden. He took the Swedish Soprano, Jenny Lind, to dinner, and discovered an "affinity between Slavs and Scandinavians". He played at Stafford House, the stronghold of the Tory aristocracy, for Queen Victoria and the Prince Consort,

and with great success elsewhere. But not with the Philharmonic, because it was "like their turtle soup, energetic, but nothing more. . . ." Furthermore, "in this country, where time is money," the orchestra rehearsed only once, and in public. Instead, he started giving lessons again, at the rate of one gold guinea a session. Again he had his own carriage waiting at the door. He also had a friend, James Broadwood, who was as solicitous as Fontana. "One evening, upon coming home, I found a new mattress and very soft pillows. . . . It was only after much insistence that I was able to persuade Daniel to tell me that they had been sent by Broadwood, who knew of my insomnia and had enjoined him to say nothing to me. . . ." Chopin led a very active social life. He met Dickens, Carlyle, Hogarth, Walter Scott. He allowed himself to be made much of by the ladies ("Lady Byron . . . how well I understand why her husband lives abroad!"). But, behind the brilliant façade: "If only I could leave off spitting blood for a while, if only I weren't a prey to an idiotic homesickness. . . . I vegetate, simply, and patiently await my end. . . ."

In April, 1848, when Chopin was already quite ill, he went to London. The drawing rooms of high society were thrown wide open for his "paid performances". He gave his first concert at 99 Eaton Place, the house of Mrs. Adelaide Sartoris, daughter of the famous actor, Kemble (500 tickets at a guinea apiece were sold); then he played at Lord Falmouth's house, 2 St. James' Square (left): "A great lover of music and a great lord; nonetheless one would be tempted to give him alms were one to meet him in the street; and at home also, he has a multitude of servants better dressed than he. . . ." He also performed at the Duchess of Sutherland's, where he was again acclaimed by the Atheneum. Only the critic of The Times, Davison, who thought Chopin a threat to his idol Mendelssohn, withheld his praise; he was later to make amends in a perceptive Essay on the Polish musician's art. Below: Regent Street, the heart of elegant London. Opposite page, from left: Walter Scott and Dickens, who admired Chopin.

London: The Italian Opera House in 1828 (below, in an etching by Shepard). Chopin appeared on November 16, 1848 at a concert and ball given at the Guildhall in the British capital for the benefit of Polish exiles (the two middle pictures on this page). It was the last time he was to appear in public. He had not wanted to disappoint Lord Stuart, president of the Association of the Friends of Poland. Bottom of page: View of Buckingham Palace. Opposite page: One aspect of English life in his day: Queen Victoria visits Somerset House.

THE HAUNTED SCOTTISH CASTLE

In Calder House, 12 miles from Edinburgh, a huge room was set aside for Chopin; on the floor above, 300 years earlier, John Knox had prayed through the night. There was a Broadwood piano in his room. In the room next to his there was a Pleyel piano, sent by Jane Stirling. There was also, inevitably, a family ghost. But the musician, who spent a portion of the summer as Lord Thorpichen's guest of honour, was not to be disturbed. In the evenings Chopin played old Scottish airs for the master of the house, a member of the Stirling clan. And "he expressed his feelings to him in French." Calder House may well have been the most satisfying

lap of his British trip: galleries, acres of lawns, horses, almost like an Antonin Castle transplanted from Poland to Scotland. But it was useless to deceive oneself. From the haven where Miss Stirling would have liked to keep the beloved master, Chopin wrote to Fontana, "I haven't a single musical idea; I am like a donkey at a masked ball." And also: "We are two old cymbals on which time and circumstance have played their dismal tremolo . . . we can't give out new notes under clumsy hands, and we choke down in ourselves all that which, for the want of an expert lute player, no one can draw out of us. . . ."

A BUNCH OF VIOLETS

Chopin was dying of depression in Scotland, despite his host's kindness. He was never again to hear from his irreplaceable "lute player"—George Sand—after his wretched meeting with her at the door of Mme Marliani's house. And Jane Stirling could give him no strength; on the contrary, she sought it from him. After barely three weeks, Chopin left Calder House. The tour he took seemed calculated to finish him off. He played in Manchester and in Glasgow. With a flash of his old spirit, he tried to keep Osborne from coming to hear him in the concert hall in Edinburgh: "I should like to leave you with the impression I made on you in Paris. . . ." Finally, in the autumn, he returned to London, where he seldom left his bed. Mrs. Erskine, Jane Stirling's sister, used to read him the Psalms, observing that "the next world is certainly better than this one." "One more day here," Chopin wrote to Grzymala, "and I shall go mad. My Scottish ladies exasperate me so." Queen Victoria's personal physician, Sir James Clark, was by now also attending him. Finally Chopin made up his mind: He wrote to Grzymala, "Order a bunch of violets for Friday, so that I may still find a little poetry when I come back. . . ."

Below: Photograph of Chopin taken a few months before his death; the ravages of sickness are evident. The Manchester Guardian *wrote, after the concert he gave on August 30, 1848: "He is very spare in frame, and there is an almost painful air of feebleness in his appearance and gait." Right: Alessio Jelowicki, a fellow student of Chopin's.*

"HE WAS AS HANDSOME AS EVER"

"I had gone to see him, and I was about to leave, because I was told that he was sleeping. When it was known who I was," reports Norwid, the poet, "Chopin asked me to come up again. . . . In the shadow of the bed hangings he was as handsome as ever, there was something sculptural about him. . . . As he greeted me, he said: 'I shall move,' and he began to cough. I replied: 'You move like this every year, and always, thank Heaven, we find you alive.' And, disregarding the coughing, he continued: 'No, I tell you, I'll move from here to go to the Place Vendôme. . . .' "

Chopin kept his word. He lived at 12 Place Vendôme from October 1 to 17, 1849. The months before this move fled by, in preparation for the end. After a painful winter, the month of May saw a deceptive improvement in his health. He had reached the highest peak of his artistry, composing luminous music—the Barcarolle, the Berceuse—which conjured up no ghosts, no hint of death. He struggled on to the very end with his customary insouciance. In June, he moved to Chaillot, where he could look upon green grass and trees. It was as close a substitute for past summers at Nohant as he could afford, for his funds were very low. The house was spacious and airy: "Besides the gardens I can see before me all of Paris, the Tuileries, Nortre Dame, St. Etienne, the Invalides . . ." Paris was still his favourite place of exile. The good weather saw him up and around again, elegant as always. He went to the Bois with Norwid, and was once more seen in Polish circles. He questioned Mickiewicz, who was back from Italy, and wrangled with Slowacki, the author of *Lilla Weneda* ("that peacock, that fool"), was to die the same year. He went to the theatre, to shudder conscientiously at the premiere of Meyerbeer's *Prophet*. And, while cholera raged (Kalkbrenner was a victim), he had a friend read to him from Voltaire's *Dictionnaire Philosophique*. Many friends came to call: Léo, Pleyel, Mme Kalergi, his last pupil, the enchantress Delphine. And, in August, he was overjoyed by the arrival of his sister, Louise, who came rushing from Warsaw to be by his side.

Left: The drawing room of 12 Place Vendôme; Chopin died there, on October 17, 1849, of tuberculosis of the larynx and the lungs. Liszt wrote of Chopin's Preludes: "Admirable in their diversity, and in the work and knowledge they reveal, they can only be appreciated after painstaking examination. Everything seems to be a first flush, an impulse, a sudden rush. They have the freedom and breath which characterize works of genius." Above: The Gare St. Lazare in 1848.

In contrast to the squalid funeral of Chopin's idol Mozart, the Polish musician's was almost a social event: About 3,000 people were present, including musical and literary society, ladies of fashion, and the English and French press. "Nature had a festive air," reporters wrote. Mozart's Requiem was sung, according to Chopin's wish, by Mme Viardot Garcia and Lablache in the Church of the Madeleine. It was a dazzling performance: "How the master would have appreciated it," the admiring chronicler of the Illustration Française wrote. Chopin was buried in the Père Lachaise cemetery. A handful of Polish soil acompanied him into the French earth. Jane Stirling saw to everything. The woman who was aptly described as "Chopin's widow" came to Père Lachaise the following year in complete privacy. She was one of the few who appreciated the funeral monument made by Clésinger. Below: Chopin's death, by Kniatowski.

"SUBLIME SONG OF ALL SUFFERING"

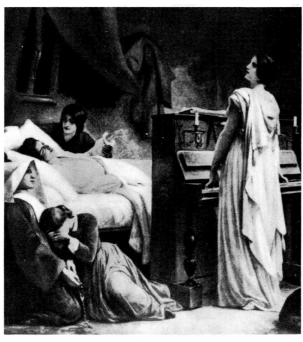

The years between 1840 and 1845 marked the high point of Chopin's artistic productivity. He was then living with George Sand, who, with her children, had given him the illusion of having a home. Among the first works of this period were: the Sonata in B Flat Minor Op. 35; the Impromptu in F Sharp Major Op. 36; the Scherzo Op. 39; the Polonaises in A Flat, in C Minor, in F Sharp Minor; the Fantaisie Op. 49; the Nocturne in G Minor. The Sonata Op. 35 was a departure from the sonata form established by Beethoven, which had once been considered the ultimate development of the form. It was disconcerting for Chopin's contemporaries; Schumann called it "the smile of the sphinx". "The idea of calling it a sonata is a caprice, if not a jest, for he has simply bound together four of his most reckless children." Especially "reckless" were the last two movements: the *marche funèbre,* and the tumultuous finale, a relentless demented presto, one of the most personal, bizarre poems ever dedicated by a romantic to death. It contains everything: anguish, demonism, sarcasm and even a touch of the baroque; "winds of night sweeping over church-

yard graves" was Anton Rubinstein's description. "Chopin," said Legouvé, "never refused to play it, but hardly was the last bar finished, than he used to reach for his hat and leave. . . ." "Out of balance" in the opinion of some, the sonata is undeniably one of the most suggestive pieces of music ever written. Pianists have not always known how to interpret it. Some, with an extraordinary talent for identifying themselves with the music, succeed in literally galvanizing the audience with this sonata. Others dominate it with an interpretation that is almost starched, unyielding, peremptory and eloquent. The Sonata in B minor Op. 57, composed in 1845, is in complete contrast to this "poem of death", which was described by Ganche as the "sublime song of all suffering, the desperate hymn of a dying world". The later Sonata Op. 58 is rather the work of a romantic who adores the classics, who, as he gradually approaches death, refuses to dramatize it, and rises disdainfully above it; it is lighter, less agonized. Developed in classical style, it is alien to the kind of romantic suffering and macabre fantasies that could drive someone like Schumann to despair.

Chopin, standing in the centre, is surrounded by well-known pianists of his day. From the left, standing: Rosenhain, Dohler, Chopin, Dreyschock, Thalberg; seated: Wolff, Henselt, Liszt. It was Paganini who taught the pianists a new technique for virtuosity on the piano, an instrument ideally suited to romanticism. Alfred Einstein wrote: "Transposing his virtuoso techniques to their instrument, the pianists—from Chopin to Liszt, to Schumann, to Brahms— tried to eliminate the normal differences between piano and violin techniques."

Much has been written on Chopin, and his figure has been variously illuminated from time to time. Actually, Chopin was an introverted genius whose music was highly individual and personal. He cared nothing for setting patterns or devising formulas for the production of universal works of art of the type in which Wagner excelled. Chopin's contribution to the evolution of music is nonetheless great. His work in harmony is the basis for much modern orchestration. He was an intensely lyrical composer who gave free rein to self-expression. He was thought by some to be out of his element in compositions of large scope, such as the concerto. Fortunately, he knew his limitations, and confined the greater part of his work to the smaller forms: nocturnes, études, preludes, dances (polonaises, mazurkas, waltzes). It was in these that he found the happiest expression of the genius, and it is no doubt one of the reasons for the popularity of his music for drawing-room playing. Despite the often strongly pronounced Polish national characteristics of his music, it is also expressive of his own emotions and sufferings, and thereby achieves the universality characteristic of any true masterpiece. Debussy said that Chopin evades "the game of classifications". He does, indeed, rise above historic or aesthetic categories, for his music has the formal perfection, clarity and balance of classicism, while at the same time it reveals the inspired vision and inner mystery of the human heart.

1810—February 22: Born at Zelazowa Wola, near Warsaw: second child of Nicolas Chopin, native of Marainville in Lorraine, teacher of French, and of Justine Krzyzanowska, a Polish lady. He had three sisters: Ludwika (Louise), Isabelle, Emily.

1811—Franz Liszt is born in Doborjàn, Hungary.

1815—After three previous partitions in 1772, 1793 and 1795, Poland is once more dismembered by the Russians, the Prussians and the Austrians.

1818—February 24: Chopin, aged eight, gives his first concert in Warsaw.

1823—Studies harmony and counterpoint with Josef Elsner, who is also to be his teacher at the Warsaw Conservatory until 1829.

1826—August: Short stay in Reinertz, a small spa in Silesia, where his sister Emily is taking a cure. She dies of consumption the following year.

1829—August: Chopin gives two concerts in Vienna. Back in Warsaw, he starts work again on his Concerto in E minor and on some of his études.

1830—March 17, March 22, October 11: He gives three concerts before leaving Poland. He is restless because of his love for Costantia Gladkowska, a young singer he has met at the Conservatory, and for whom he composes the Larghetto of Concerto Op. 21 and the Waltz Op. 70. November 2, All Saints Day: Frédéric Chopin leaves Poland forever. Homesickness for his native land (he takes with him a fistful of Polish soil in a silver box) is to stay with him for the whole of his life. In November,

Warsaw rises up against the autocracy of Czar Nicholas I of Russia.

1831—September 8: The Russians, under the command of General Paskievic, reoccupy Warsaw. Mid-September: Chopin settles in Paris, after spending almost nine months in Vienna and two months in various German cities.

1832—February and March: Two concerts at the Salle Pleyel reveal Chopin's greatness to the élite of Paris. Finishes the Etudes Op. 10. From this year until 1836, he composes, among other pieces, Scherzo Op. 20, Ballade Op. 23, Rondo Op. 16, Mazurkas Op. 24, Nocturnes Op. 27.

1835—Sees his parents again at Karlsbad, where they have gone to take the cure. Then, in Dresden, he sees Maria Wodzinska, his first piano pupil in Warsaw, for whom he has always had a deep affection. He composes the Valse d' Adieu for her. He plays with Hiller and Liszt in various concerts.

1836—Summer: Chopin asks for the hand of Maria Wodzinska, but the following autumn he receives through her mother a veiled refusal from the girl. The reason for this is the apprehension of Maria's parents about Chopin's precarious health. November: First meeting with George Sand, in the Liszt household.

1837—Brief stay in London with Camille Pleyel.

1838—November: Chopin and Sand in the Balearic Islands. They live first in Palma di Majorca in the villa Son Vent, then at the Chartreuse di Valdemosa. Here he composes the 24 Preludes, Scherzo Op. 39, Im-

promptu Op. 36, Polonaise Op. 40, Mazurkas Op. 41.

1839—June: Because of the inclement weather. Chopin returns to France and spends the summer in Nohant at Sand's home. He is to return here for successive summers, spending the winters in Paris. Composes Sonata B flat minor Op. 35—which contains the famous *Marche Funèbre*—a nocturne and four mazurkas.

1841—April 26: Another concert at the Salle Pleyel in Paris, this time as soloist. Liszt writes an enthusiastic review. Chopin's health, meantime, continues to deteriorate, but he nonetheless goes through a period of intense inspiration and composes his Polonaise in A major, Ballade in A flat major, three mazurkas and two nocturnes. These are some of his most important works.

1844—A sad year: The death of his father, the advance of his disease, quarrels with George Sand.

1847—August: Break with George Sand.

1848—February 12: Chopin's last concert in Paris. April: At the insistence of one of his admirers, the Scottish lady Jane Stirling, he crosses the Channel and gives, in London and in other cities in England and Scotland, his last concerts.

1849—October 17: Death of Frédéric Chopin in Paris. Before the end he asks his older sister Louise (who has been present at his death bed) to take his heart back to Poland. The mortal remains of the great musician are buried, at his request, in the Pere Lachaise cemetery in Paris, not far from the graves of Bellini and Cherubini.